LEWES

THEN and NOW

High Street, Cliffe,   Lewes.

Bill Young
in association with
Bob Cairns

S.B. Publications

Previous Titles
Bill Young: *Line of Fire – a History of Firefighting in Lewes* (1996)
Bob Cairns: *Lewes in Old Picture Postcards* (1988)

First published in 1998 by S B Publications
c/o 19 Grove Road, Seaford, Sussex BN25 1TP

© 1998 Bill Young
Reprinted 1999

ISBN 1 85770 144 5

Typeset by JEM Lewes
Printed and bound by The Adland Print Group Ltd.
Unit 11, Bellingham Trading Estate, Franthorne Way, London SE6 3BX.

ACKNOWLEDGMENTS

I am indebted to Barbara Fleming for permission to reprint the two maps used in her book *Lewes – Two Thousand Years of History* (SB Publications); to Joyce Crow and Richard Philcox of Sussex Archaeological Society for their many kindnesses; and to Ken Head for his research work. I am also grateful to Steve Sullivan, the Crowborough photographer, for copying the postcards. In particular, I am indebted to Bob Cairns, for generous access to his postcard collection.

BIBLIOGRAPHY

Colin Brent: *Historic Lewes and its Buildings,* Lewes Town Council, 1985
Colin Brent and William Rector: *Victorian Lewes,* Phillimore, 1980
Bob Cairns: *Lewes in Old Picture Postcards,* European Library, Zattbommel, 1988
Alec Clifton-Taylor: *Six More English Towns,* BBC, 1981
LS Davey: *The Street Names of Lewes* (revised edition), Lewes Town Council, 1981
Barbara Fleming: *Lewes – Two Thousand Years of History,* SB Publications, 1994
Kelly's Street Directories of Lewes

INTRODUCTION

THE charm of Lewes and its situation has been recognised by many writers over the years. As long ago as 1724, Daniel Defoe, author of Robinson Crusoe, Moll Flanders and many other books described Lewes as a 'fine pleasant town, well built, agreeably situated in the middle of an open champaign country'. About two hundred years later, Thomas Horsfield, the Unitarian Minister of Lewes's Westgate Chapel, commented: 'Although on an elevated site, it is yet encircled by an amphitheatre of loftier hills, which give to it a truly picturesque and pleasant character.' Later in the nineteenth century, William Morris wrote: 'You can see Lewes lying like a box of toys under a green amphitheatre of chalk hills. On the whole, it is set down better than any other town I have seen in England.'

More recently, the late Alec Clifton-Taylor, in his second volume of studies of English towns (1981), looked at Lewes and its architecture. He wrote: 'Lewes has for me a twofold appeal. There is the old town itself, bestraddling its chalky crest and spilling down the slopes, with its abundant legacy of flint, tiles and brick. And there is the setting, of which surely the fortunate citizens never grow tired: that glorious Downland landscape with the clean line of hills silhouetted against the sky.'

Visitors to the town as well as Lewesians would agree that all these authors could not have been wrong. I like these words from a modern hymn which seems to me to have been penned with Lewes in mind.

I lift my eyes to the quiet hills
In the press of a busy day
As green hills stand in a dusty land
So God is my strength and stay.

Life in Lewes today, as in so many other historical towns and cities, is marked by noise, clamour and change. How many generations of Lewesians and visitors to the town, have looked to the Downs and found peace and tranquility, drawing strength from their solid form, shape and continuity.

In addition to the beauty of both the town and its setting, Lewes is privileged in two other respects. Firstly, Edward Reeves lived in Lewes and established a still-thriving photographic business at 159 High Street, next to St Michael's Church. His career spanned the years from 1854 until his death in 1905. Reeves' camera recorded physical changes to the town and its buildings as well as its social structure and history in photographs of high technical quality and empathic artistry. Largely because the business passed to his son, then grandson and now great-grandson, Tom, Lewes has a wonderful photographic legacy of its past and I am pleased to have been able to use photographs from the Reeves collection in this book.

Secondly, Bob Cairns, a Ringmer resident and postcard collector, has amassed a collection of some 1,800 postcards of Lewes, providing another fascinating insight into life in the town, and he made his collection available for this book. Many of the cards have not previously been published.

In a book of this size, I have been limited to fewer than fifty photographs of Lewes *Then*. With the wealth of material available, the most difficult exercise has been to decide what to include and what to leave out and I make no apology, therefore, that I have included photographs which are my own particular favourites.

The photographs of Lewes *Now* are my own. The aim has been to try to take them from as close to the position taken up by the original photographer as possible. However, given the nature of some of the changes in road patterns, and in the amount and speed of modern traffic, this has sometimes been impossible. Modern 35mm cameras and lenses are also quite different from the cameras and lenses that would have been used by Edward Reeves. This also has meant that sometimes the views do not match exactly.

Bill Young
1998

THEN – ASTLEY HOUSE: This Edward Reeves photograph shows the corner of Spital Road and Western Road around the turn of the century. Astley House, was the home of George Poole, one of Lewes's most famous race horse trainers. It is said that his yard was probably the best in Lewes with the horse boxes being arranged in a rough horseshoe. Further along Spital Road, on the site recently occupied by Western Road Primary School, once stood the hospitium of St Nicholas, the original purpose of which was to provide hospitality to pilgrims and travellers. The remains of this building were converted into cottages that were demolished in 1933 to provide space for school extensions.

NOW: The scene is now dominated by two unattractive buildings. One (left centre) is the St Pancras Church's Canon O'Donnel Community Centre and the other (right), a building used by the Sussex Police Authority for various purposes. Before its conversion to police use, the building was Mansfield's Garage. Western Road School, which is just out of sight, is now the St Nicholas Centre, run by East Sussex County Council. The gable end of the Windmill public house can be seen above the road sign.

THEN – ST ANNE'S HILL: Another Edward Reeves photograph shows St Anne's Church in about 1870. The Pelham Arms probably dates from Stuart times, and may well have been The Rose. It later became The Dog and acquired its present name about 1790. It was, of course, named after the Pelham family who owned it for many years. The inn was well known to the racing fraternity and its extensive stabling was used by trainers when they visited the town for race meetings.

NOW: Except for parked cars and an improved road surface, the scene has changed very little in one hundred and twenty years.

THEN – ST ANNE'S HILL: This old postcard is believed to show Lord John Sanger's Circus in 1907. The parade is opposite what was then St Anne's Post Office – the shop is now a gunsmith's, the Lewes Gun Room. The occupier, Mr GT Baker, as well as running the post office, also owned the baker's shop at 45 Western Road. Below the post office is the Morning Star public house, while above it is the stable block for the Pelham Arms Hotel.

NOW: The Morning Star was, until fairly recently, the Bow Windows Bookshop – which has now moved lower down the High Street. The former pub is now a private residence. The Pelham Arms stable block subsequently became a garage until its demolition and redevelopment as Well House Place.

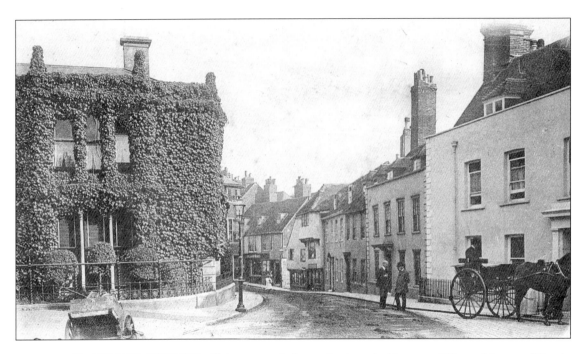

THEN – ST ANNE'S CORNER: This postcard shows the ivy-clad house of Henry Newson Woods shortly after the turn of the century. What is now the Fifteenth Century Bookshop was occupied by Miss Pettitt, costumier, while on the other side of Keere Street was the Montpelier Laundry Company's office at 98, Thomas Riekie, butcher, 97 and Robert Barber Company, bookbinders, 96. The elegant buildings on the right of this photograph were all private residences.

NOW: The former ivy-clad building at 143 now houses the Lewes YMCA and the Southdowns Council for Voluntary Service. The private residences form an attractive group of buildings with their good state of repair and their colour washed walls. Number 96 is now Full of Beans, while 97, at the time this photograph was taken, was for sale.

THEN – WESTGATE STREET: At the time this photograph was thought to have been taken (c1875), the firm of William and William Pannett, hay, straw, corn and coal merchants, had been established seventy years. It operated from the railway wharf and 216 High Street and, by the late 1880s, had extended its business to include premises in Westgate Street and then Friars Walk. By the beginning of World War One the firm was operating as a coal merchants only.

NOW: The Westgate premises, a well-restored group of period commercial buildings, are now used by building contractor Philcox Brothers Limited, and by Westgate Joinery.

THEN– KEERE STREET: The street name appears in a deed dated 1272 as 'the path called Kerestrete'. Keere Street is a much sought after address but at one time it was very different and much less salubrious. Half way down the hill can be seen the sign of the Britannia Inn which stood at number 9, and which was closed by the licensing authorities in the 1920s. The photograph was taken outside the premises of Pinyoun, baker and grocer from about the turn of the century until the 1940s. The children in their white overdresses with the hoops and the doll's pram make a charming group.

NOW: Largely unchanged, Keere Street still retains many of its old blue cobblestones with which most of Lewes's streets were once paved.

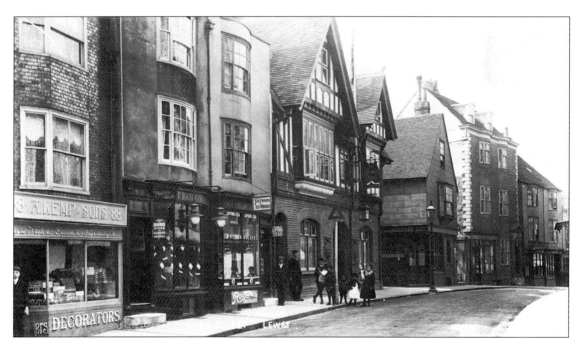

THEN – HIGH STREET: This picture shows the still thriving commercial area towards the top of the town. Number 88 was Kemps, plumber and bird preserver – a strange combination! At 89 there was Briggs, tailor and breeches maker while next door was Willoughby's tea rooms and confectionery business. The Brewers Arms, 91, was formerly The Ship, a name which is believed to have had religious connotations, possibly symbolising the Ark as a place of shelter. It was rebuilt about the turn of the century. Next to the pub is Bull House, which at that time was a reading room, while at 93, Mrs Annie Plummer traded as a draper.

NOW: Although the thriving commercial heart of the town may have shifted to the Cliffe, this part of the High Street is still busy. At 88, Lucy of Lewes provided *Cordon Bleu* catering for many years until the business closed in July 1998. Number 89 is The Treasury, specialising in small antiques, while at 90 is the Lewes Gallery. Beyond the Brewers Arms is Bull House, headquarters of the Sussex Archaeological Society, from where Thomas Paine once ran a tobacconist and snuff shop, Westgate Chapel and Westgate House.

THEN – CASTLE PLACE, HIGH STREET: Castle Place (165-167) began life as a terrace of four houses but the middle two were later combined into a single dwelling for Gideon Mantell, the celebrated geologist and discoverer of the iguandon. The house, with its distinctive ironwork and with the ammonite capitals that were the designer's trade-mark, was built in around 1810 by Amon Wilds and his son, Amon Henry. The Wilds moved to Brighton in 1820 where, with Charles Augustin Busby, they designed most of Kemp Town together with Montpelier Crescent and Park Crescent.

NOW: Castle Place is still elegant and distinctive and has not been spoiled by the removal of the bay window. The latter was probably a late Victorian addition. The properties are now occupied by The Guild of Master Craftsmen.

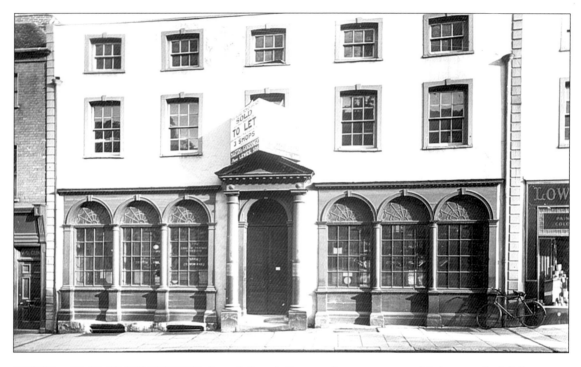

THEN – 61-62 HIGH STREET: Lowdell and Cooper, ironmongers, with its wonderful frontage, was established in 1812 providing 'everything for house, farm or garden'. The company sold both trade and retail and later described itself as 'builders merchants'. It seems that by 1937, it had given up 61 and concentrated its business at 62. MacFisheries had taken over the shop by 1939. Joseph Molyneux, who controlled the Maresfield forge, was apparently responsible for the fine iron shop front shown in the photograph. The frontage was subsequently removed.

NOW: This is one of Lewes's saddest present day sights and one that needs urgent attention. There has been some improvement with the opening of The Wine Cellar's premises, but with the iron shop front having gone, even the fine doorway has been neglected and is in danger of decay.

High Street & County Hall.   Lewes.

THEN – HIGH STREET (THE OLD COUNTY HALL): This delightful building was erected in 1812 and was faced in Portland stone. It served as the county council's main administrative offices until 1968 when the new County Hall was built. The old Town Hall and Sessions House, which stood in the middle of the High Street between the White Hart and the old County Hall, was demolished in 1801. Number 182, here occupied by Davey, a saddler, was formerly Newcastle House, owned by the Duke of Newcastle.

NOW: The old County Hall was extended in 1930 and, with the opening of the new Magistrates' Court in Friars Walk in 1986, was refurbished and re-designated as the Lewes Combined Court. In 1929 Newcastle House was incorporated into an extension of the old County Hall.

THEN – 53 HIGH STREET:
George Coppard and Son, fish-mongers and poulterers, ran their business from these premises from at least 1874, and Coppard and Likeman were in partnership well before the turn of the century. By the outbreak of World War One, they were describing themselves as Coppard and Likeman's Fish, Poultry and Ice Stores trading at these same premises at 53 High Street next door to the old Boots the Chemist shop. The shop survived until about 1962. This photograph was evidently taken at Christmas some time after the change of name. Note the woman cleaning the windows next door. Mrs Pelling at 54 was a boot and shoe maker and she shared premises with the Lewes Conservative Association, the Primrose League and the Gundreda Habitation.

NOW: The old Boots the Chemist building is now occupied by The Shoe Gallery and Bridal Fayre. The former Coppard and Likeman premises are now The Drawing Room, an antiques shop, while the building occupied by Mrs Pelling is now used by Forbuoys newsagents.

THEN – HIGH STREET (WHITE HART HOTEL): Originally, the White Hart Hotel was the town house of the powerful Pelhams before they moved to Pelham House in St Andrew's Lane. It became a coaching inn around 1717. Next door is the Unicorn Inn, a small public house previously known as the Three Pelicans. Next to the Unicorn at 57-58 High Street is Mrs Stephen's restaurant and tea rooms while beyond the White Hart is bootmaker John Hoad, at 54A, King and Son, antique furniture, 54 and, at 53, Coppard and Likeman.

NOW: Two hundred and eighty years on, the White Hart Hotel serves the motorist rather than stage-coach passengers. The building that was once the Unicorn Inn is now the long-established Wycherley family estate agency business. Beyond the White Hart is Forbuoys newspaper shop, 54, The Drawing Room antiques shop, 53, Bridal Fayre, 52, The Shoe Gallery, 51 and on the corner of the High Street and Station Street, at 50, is the Abbey National.

THEN – HIGH STREET (SCHOOL HILL): The Georgian building featured in the Reeves photograph was once the coach office when the Star Inn, now the Town Hall, was the district's coaching centre – or at least, so says an advertisement in an old Lewes guide. In 1849, Messrs Stevenson, tea merchants from Brighton, opened this branch in Lewes. After a few years, the shop changed hands, ceased its Brighton connection and was acquired by TG Roberts in the 1870s. Roberts also had a branch at 28 Western Road. Mr Roberts can be seen peering out of his doorway. The shop at 45-46 continued to operate under the name TG Roberts until about 1966.

NOW: The building has changed hands a number of times in the last century. In 1966, it became the International Tea Company Stores, then the International Stores and then, briefly, Gateway Foodmarket. Workmen clearing the building before conversion to its present use found the original kitchen range in the cellar and a six feet high tapestry made from glued copies of the 1887 *Young Ladies Journal* secured to the attic wall under several layers of wallpaper. The building now houses Unicorn Books and a shoe repairer.

THEN – HIGH STREET (TOWN HALL): The Town Hall was reconstructed in 1893 from The Star Inn. Parts of the old building were incorporated in the conversion, including the cellars. The splendid Elizabethan carved staircase was acquired in 1760 from a derelict mansion, Slaugham Place, near Cuckfield. Beyond, at 186, can be seen the sign of C Morrish and Son, founded around 1880. Shortly after the turn of the century, it was known as the Lewes Drapers Emporium. Between Morrish and the Town Hall stood the boot and shoe premises of Albion Russell, whose daughter married GF Bromley in 1847, creating the firm of Russell and Bromley.

NOW: By the 1960s, the shop was called Morrish's Macartney Stewart, drapers and, later in the 1960s, Macartney Stewart. At the time of this photograph the shop was empty and for sale. For some years the building has been in a poor state of repair and an eyesore on one of the most prominent corners in the town. The Tourist Information Centre, on the opposite side of Fisher Street, was the first Russell and Bromley shoe shop in Britain. The War Memorial was built in 1922, replacing the rather ornate three branch street lamp.

THEN – ALBION STREET:
Albion Street was laid out in 1822 by the builder James Berry and Son (who took over the Lewes business of Amon Wild) when a new road was cut from School Hill to East Street (then known as Poplar Row). The long balconied terrace on the west side of Albion Street presents a charming picture. Until then, a large Tudor residence standing in extensive grounds had occupied the whole site. Originally known as the Turk's Head Inn (1678), it later became the residence of Dr Thomes Frewin, a pioneer in inoculation against smallpox, and later still, a school.

NOW: On the left of the photograph is Berkeley House Hotel at number 2, while further down is the Albion Street Dental Practice at 7. Opposite the hotel is the premises of Clifford Dann, surveyor, valuer and estate agent, built in the mid-1960s and sadly out of place opposite this elegant terrace of houses. The Kingdom Hall of the Jehovah's Witnesses was demolished to make way for this building and car park. At the end of Albion Street stands the local library. This once incorporated the museum.

SCHOOL HILL, LEWES.

THEN – HIGH STREET (SCHOOL HILL): This 1912 view of School Hill, before the War Memorial was built, shows Freeman Hardy and Willis's boot and shoe shop at 36 and Baxter's printing works and the Sussex Express offices at 35. At 35A was the Vinall, Launcelot boy's school and just before Walwers Lane, at 34, E&C Cruttenden (pastry cooks). Beyond can be seen School Hill House and Lewes House. On the other side of the road was AF Atkinson, stationer, at 193, Nelson's domestic machine depot at 194, Farrow's Bank, 195, Montague Fuller, dentist, 196 and the Co-Op Boot Stores and Leather Sellers Society at 197.

NOW: Lewes House (headquarters of Lewes District Council) and School Hill House (a doctors' practice) still dominate the scene in a pleasing way. At 36 is Farrago with Fogdens, men's outfitters next door at 37. Sussex Stationers and Breedons Bookshop share 34 and Caburn Communications are at 35. On the opposite side of the road, Fox and Sons, estate agents, occupy 192, with Lyons newsagents at 193, Brats, children's clothes, at 194 and Deckerway, a betting shop, at 195.

THEN – HIGH STREET-EASTGATE STREET JUNCTION: William Crosskey, a Unitarian churchman, owned this draper's and general outfitter's shop (established in 1789) at the junction of the High Street, Eastgate Street and Friars Walk. The shop was built on the sight of Holy Trinity Church, close to the medieval town's east gate. The church was demolished as long ago as 1319 because of its ruinous state. William Crosskey also operated a furniture store in Friars Walk in a building which, much later, became Courts, a furniture shop. This was destroyed by fire in November 1973. The façade of Eastgate Stoneworks can be seen in the distance behind the horse chestnut tree.

NOW: The positioning of the camera suggests that little has changed in the hundred years since the first photograph was taken. But, with the building of the Eastgate development and the Safeway Superstore and, on the other side of Eastgate Street, the much earlier bus station (1950s), there has been wide scale change.

THEN – HIGH STREET (SCHOOL HILL): This timeless photograph, with a flock of sheep being herded down the middle of an empty School Hill, was taken as Lewes was preparing for Coronation Day on June 22, 1911. The sign of the Singer Sewing Machine Company, at 18 can be seen on the left. This firm shared premises with the Misses Cockrom and Holder (fancy drapers) while the Lewes Savings Bank, 16, conducted its business from the building below. Above Singer's were John Fuller (draper) at 19; the wine vaults of Harvey and Son at 19A; Caleb Mitchell (general drapers) at 20-21; the Misses Hickson's Ladies School, 22, and Carvill's and Huggett's shops at 24 and 25.

NOW: Driving a flock of sheep down School Hill today would be an act of suicide! The music shop, Octave, is at 18, Glynde Gardens florist's shop at 19, The Training Consortium at 20, Luggage Plus at 22 and Emporium Antiques at 24. Lower down, Jumpers, 16, occupies what was once the Lewes Savings Bank.

THEN – FRIARS WALK: This handsome building was Lewes's first railway terminal and was completed by the London, Brighton and South Coast Railway Company in 1846. The location of the station meant that some very complex manoeuvres were needed by trains and this was one of the reasons for the building of a new station in 1857 which was located near the present station.

NOW: The former Railway Inn, which closed in the 1960s, was clearly built to cater for passengers arriving at the nearby railway station. It is now private residential flats. Fitzroy House peers through the trees (left) and, just as the station terminal dominated the 1860s photograph, so the new Magistrates' Court, built in 1986 by GL James, imposes itself on the present scene.

THEN – LOWER HIGH STREET: This striking Independent Congregational church, the Tabernacle, with its large classical portico, was built in 1816 and enlarged in 1832. It could seat 1,200 worshippers. Charles Aspull Wells, a local pioneer of electricity, owned the shop to the left of the Tabernacle. The Tabernacle's Sunday School building, which still stands in Railway Lane on the former Etna ironwork's site (also owned by Charles Wells), could take 500 children.

NOW: The Tabernacle was demolished in the early/mid 1950s and replaced by an unimaginative and charmless block of shops. In the 1980s the lower part of High Street was redeveloped as a pedestrian precinct with brick-faced shop units on either side. The shop to the left of the old Tabernacle still stands. After many years as Rice Brothers, a saddlery, it is now owned by Forfars' bakery chain.

THEN – HIGH STREET LOOKING EAST: This Cheetham's postcard (c1910) shows the Seveirg building (supposedly the name of the builder, Grieves, in reverse) on the corner of Eastgate and the railway bridge which carried the line to Uckfield. The latter was axed in about 1969 to allow the building of Phoenix Causeway to take through traffic out of Cliffe High Street, and the bridge came down a year or so later.

NOW: Neither the Clifford Dann building (on the corner of High Street and Albion Street), which is out of place in a generally elegant part of the High Street, nor the Eastgate development, with its architectural cliches, improves this view of the High Street. Cuilfail is seen on Cliffe Hill beyond.

THEN– CLIFFE BRIDGE: The business of JCH Martin was established in 1904 in these premises which were originally purpose built in the 1880s by Albion Russell as a shoe manufactory. Martin also had branches in Crowborough and Lindfield. The rapid progress of the firm meant that it also acquired the building on the other side of the river where once stood the Bear Hotel, destroyed by fire in 1918. The workshops were equipped for every aspect of vehicle repair – electrical, tyres, cellulose, trimming, bodywork, high pressure oiling and greasing 'by skilled mechanics'.

NOW: The firm survived until the 1940s when the building became a garage and office premises for LA Beck, the car hire/taxi firm. The mayoral car was garaged there for some years. Recently, new life has been breathed back into these almost derelict premises with the creation of the Riverside Centre, a development of small shops, food hall and cafe.

THEN– CLIFFE HIGH STREET: The Bear Hotel, which burned down in 1918, can be seen in this evocative postcard which shows both a car and a horse and wagon on Cliffe Bridge. Beyond the Bear is Rice Brothers, saddlers, at 56-57. The Cliffe offered a number of provision merchants, boot store, draper, fruiterer, fishmongers, outfitters, tea merchants, butcher and a watchmaker/jeweller..

NOW: The photograph shows Harvey's Brewery shop shrouded in netting and scaffolding after the fire in 1996 which also damaged the Granada, Harveys, Intersport and Friday-Ad shops. The Argos shop occupies premises built on the site of the old Bear Hotel while the conversion of the former Martin's/Beck's garage to the Riverside Centre has helped breathe new life into the Cliffe.

THEN – CENTRAL NATIONAL SCHOOL: In 1811 the Church of England formed the National Society to educate the children of the poor. This Central National School was built in 1840, in Southover Road. It closed in 1938. The two stone children on the flint facade are now in Anne of Cleves House Museum. The school catered for three hundred and seventy five children of mixed sex. Southover House, built in 1938 by East Sussex County Council, as offices for its surveyor's department and, more recently, occupied by its planning department, can be seen behind the trees. This photograph must have been taken in 1938.

NOW: By 1969, the school building was used by Hammond's as a furniture repository or store. It was subsequently boarded up and virtually became derelict and was threatened with demolition. A long campaign by townsfolk to prevent demolition was successful and the building was restored in 1993 and refurbished for use by St Andrew's Surgery. Southover House was made surplus to the county council's requirements following the creation of the Brighton and Hove Unitary Authority. It has now been sold to Lewes District Council.

THEN – PRIORY CRESCENT, SOUTHOVER HIGH STREET: Ivy covers the great gate of Lewes Priory, while beyond is the splendid sweep of Priory Crescent. On the left edge of the photo-graph can be seen the shed of Thomas Goldsmith who, besides being the local wheelwright, was also parish clerk.

NOW: The view has changed little in one hundred and twenty years. The road surface has improved, there are more trees and the fact that this photograph was taken in the summer also softens the scene. The King's Head does not actually appear in either photograph but continues to dispense refreshment to the weary traveller, much as it did in 1870.

THEN – SOUTHOVER HIGH STREET: The Swan public house (partly seen on the right) was owned by William Verrall, the brewer. Next to the Swan is the forge where Samuel Hillman, blacksmith, worked. At various times, he was also Southover's Headborough, Constable and Ale-conner. Note the young lad with his milk can leaning against the forge door post.

NOW: This scene, which includes The Swan, now one of Harvey's pubs, has undergone some change since 1870. The old forge is no longer in use for that purpose, the wall to the left of the building adjacent to the forge has been demolished, and the fascia tiles of the same building have been replaced.

THEN – LEWES RAILWAY STATION: The station moved from its original site in Friars Walk to Station Road in 1857. In a contemporary publication, the new station was described as follows: 'The building is in the Gothic style and its architectural features have a very pleasing effect'. In 1889, this station gave way to the present building (shown above) which was located slightly south of the 1857 station.

NOW: In recent years, the canopy at the front entrance to the station has been renewed so that it replicates that in the 1914 postcard. Improvements to the station, the condition of which had deteriorated since it won the Ian Allan Railway Heritage Award in 1989, have been promised.

THEN – LANSDOWN PLACE LOOKING WEST: This 1909 postcard shows the National School in the background. Boots and shoes hang outside H Cottrell's boot store at number 10, while further on is William Tribe's grocer's shop at 18, the Norfolk Hotel at 32 and AM Bliss's photographic studio at 34.

NOW: Cars now line the street as they do everywhere in Lewes these days. Next to the Lansdown Arms are the Dragon House Chinese Takeaway at 34 and the Light of Bengal Indian Restaurant at 32. Lansdown Antiques and Interiors is on the corner of St Nicholas Lane. As in other parts of Lewes, traffic calming measures have been introduced in Lansdown Place.

THEN – LANSDOWN PLACE LOOKING EAST: The Lansdown Arms can be easily identified on the left of the photograph. On the opposite corner stands the New Station Inn, demolished in 1963 to give traffic better visibility. Next to the Lansdown Arms is Bliss's photographic studio, then the Norfolk Temperance Hotel. Opposite, next to the New Station Inn, was Milham's, a confectioners; then a picture frame makers run by a Mr Millet; and another confectioners, Cronins.

NOW: Next to the Lansdown Arms, on the left, are the Dragon House and the Light of Bengal. Facing the pub is Wyborn's chemist shop at number 35, and further down is Florence's, the confectioners, Academy Music and, in recent years, a number of specialist shops for which Lansdown Place has been renowned.

THEN – MALLING STREET: A number of major businesses have disappeared from the Lewes scene over the years. One of these, the Lewes Sanitary Steam Laundry Company, was destroyed by fire in March 1941. The laundry, which served Lewes and the surrounding villages, stood at the top of Malling Hill at its junction with Mill Road. The site covered a large area with the green in Mill Road used as a drying ground. The business employed dozens of staff, many of whom lived in Mill Road Villas.

NOW: A small, unattractive block of flats and a lay-by for buses now covers the site of the old Steam Laundry.

Malling Street, Lewes. II. No 742

THEN – MALLING STREET: This was once an important commercial part of the town. It is possible to pick out a couple of inn signs from this picture. On the right is The Swan, which subsequently became a laundry and then an electricity board depot; further down, on the other side, is the Dorset Arms. In the left foreground, J Shaw, grocer, had number 2 while on the other side of the road, WH Moore, draper, was at number 1. William Pocock ran a second hand market/pawnbrokers at 3, while W Butler, hairdresser, whose premises seem to have a barber's pole, was at 5.

NOW: The Dorset Arms, which for a few years changed its name to the Manxman, is once again the Dorset Arms. The former Swan Inn is now Pastorale antiques warehouse while William Pocock's shop is now occupied by Thackerys restaurant. Much of the background in the old photograph disappeared to make way for Phoenix Causeway and, later, the Cuifail Tunnel.

THEN – MALLING STREET: This atmospheric photograph is of the bottom of Malling Street, just before the First World War. The shop is T Baker, post office and confectioner, at 113. There were many small businesses in the area – a basket maker at 27, a bootmaker at 29, a fishmonger at 33, a bacon dryer at 45, a grocer at 51, farriers at 61 and at 63 was the Rock Inn. The graveyard of St Thomas a Becket, behind the wall in the middle of the picture, was removed when the road layout was changed for the construction of Phoenix Causeway.

NOW: The cottages (left foreground) numbers 115, 113, 111, 109 and 107 all survive: the cottages (right background in the previous picture) were demolished to make way for Cuilfail Tunnel (built to take through traffic out of narrow South Street). None of the small shops and businesses have survived.

THEN – MALLING STREET: Builder William Weller, who previously used a yard at 48 Malling Street, was, by this time (the early 1920s) operating from premises at number 55, and had branched out into decorating and undertaking. Bertie Putland conducted his business as a beer retailer from 62 and John French owned the house where the car is parked. W Twort, motor engineer and haulage contractor, ran the garage that can just be seen on the right. On the other side of the road was the Rock Inn at 63, Smith and Green, farriers, at 61 and Mrs Godden's general shop at 65-69.

NOW: The cottages on the left have all gone. The site of Twort's garage was, until recently, a petrol station and is now Blackwell's car show room. Again, all the small shops in the area have gone, including the well-remembered Bottle and Basket run by Mr and Mrs Evans in the 1970s.

Malling Street,

Lewes.

THEN – MALLING STREET: At 113 (right foreground) is Mrs Porter's post office and general shop, then Coombe House, owned by Albion Broad, then the ivy covered Wheatsheaf Inn, run by Joseph Rooke. Further on, at 135, stood the Tanners Arms, publican Alfred Burgess, and the former Elmsleys Brewery, by this time a mineral water manufacturing plant. On the opposite side of the road was E Russell's nursery and John Somerville and Miss Somerville, dressmaker and milliner.

NOW: All the properties on the left, including the ivy clad house with the attractive portico and the weatherboarded properties, have been demolished leaving the petrol station which was, for some years, Dixon's Garage. The old Elmsley's Brewery building, used much later by Lunnon for paper storage, was demolished after a fire and the site is now occupied by Lewes Poultry Specialists, Peter Cox Preservation and AC Sheetmetal.

THEN – NORTH STREET: This area had a number of pubs and taverns, all of which have disappeared – The Stag, the Waterloo Tavern, the King's Arms, the Blacksmith's Arms, and the Royal Marine. Edward Roswell ran the chemist's shop at number 11 Market Street (centre of picture) from about 1870 until 1883.

NOW: Number 11 Market Street is now The Pine Chest. At 18 Market Street is Fillers, a sandwich bar; Number 17 is the Patio Pizzeria and at 16 is Farncombe House, an office block. At 15 is Nigel Weller, solicitor, while George Justice, furniture restorer, operates from 12a. Cobblers, the shoe repair business, although just a few doors away is, in fact, in North Street, number 73a.

THEN – THE OLD NAVAL PRISON: This grim and forbidding building on the North Street/Lancaster Street corner was built originally in 1792 as a house of correction. It was no longer used after the new prison was built on the Brighton Road but, during the Crimean War, the building housed 400 Russian and Finnish prisoners of war captured in the Baltic. It was later used as a naval prison, and later still by the Territorial Army before being demolished in 1963.

NOW: A large car park , Lewes's ambulance station and John Springman House, the offices of the local health authority, now occupy the site.

THE EASTGATE BAPTIST CHURCH & SCHOOL, LEWES.

THEN – EASTGATE BAPTIST CHURCH: The church was built in 1818 and rebuilt in 1843. The 'pepperpot' was added when the tower was almost completed. The addition was an afterthought because someone wanted to put something on top of the tower! The Sunday School building, which can be seen on the other side of Little East Street, was opened on November 1, 1899.

NOW: In 1915, the 'pepper-pot' was found to be unsafe due to the vibration of traffic. It was removed and the upper portion of the tower rebuilt in its present pyramid shape. The Sunday School was demolished in November 1967 to make way for the Phoenix Causeway scheme. Some of the compensation money was used to build the frequently criticised new church hall abutting the front of the church. It is understood that it was the local authority of the time that insisted on the unpopular yellow bricks!

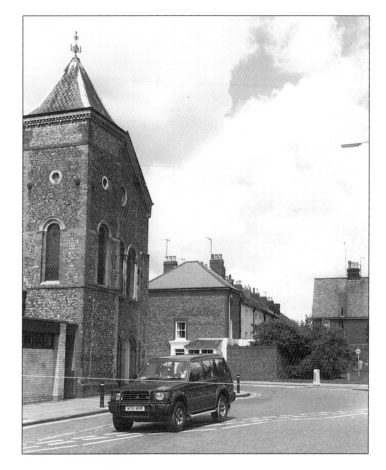

THEN – NORTH STREET: This lovely postcard shows another part of Lewes which has changed beyond all recognition and not for the better. On the right, at the junction with East Street, is the Stag Hotel.

NOW: Lewes was left largely unscathed by the bombs of the Luftwaffe in the Second World War. However, on January 20, 1943, fighter-bombers dropped high explosives on the town as well as attacking with cannon and machine gun fire. Two people were killed and there was much damage to property in North Street. A fire that evening completed the destruction of the Stag Hotel and adjoining property that had been extensively damaged by the bombing. Another car park occupies the site.

THEN – NORTH STREET: This Cheetham postcard clearly shows the old fire station and the naval prison as well as the sign of the Stag Hotel on the right. At number 3 North Street can be seen the awning of FW Curtis's grocer's shop, and at 4-5 is R Stevenson Limited, forage contractor, miller and baker.

NOW: The ivy-clad three storey terrace houses have gone to make way for the telephone exchange while the naval prison was demolished in the 1960s. The Lewes Citizen's Advice Bureau currently has its offices at number 3, while the old Stevenson's building was, until early 1998, occupied by a flea market. Stevenson's moved to Railway Lane a few years earlier.

THEN – TORONTO TERRACE: On the reverse of this postcard Nellie Readdy wrote that it is a photograph of her terrace with her 'Dada' just leaving home at 6 o'clock in the morning. Seemingly, the photographer also had an early start! From his uniform, it appears that Mr Readdy was a railway employee.

NOW: This quiet little backwater near the Pells has scarcely changed in the ninety years since the postcard photograph was taken.

THEN – NORTH STREET/LANCASTER STREET JUNCTION: A baker's shop stood here from the early 1900s until at least 1940. Firstly, WH Hall had premises at 11 North Street, then J Huggett took over the business in about 1913. Frederick Charles Huggett expanded by taking over numbers 1-3 Lancaster Street in about 1921. Finally, E Colvin acquired the business in 1931 with Charles Verrall running a fishmonger's business at 12 North Street until the 1960s.

NOW: During recent times, the premises were in use as a meeting house/church by the Jehovah's Witnesses. The building was then bought by John Lancaster and converted into two self-contained flats.

THEN – LEICESTER ROAD: This part of Lewes was an extremely busy one with many commercial activities supporting the numerous local racing stables. The corner shop was owned by George Briggs, a greengrocer and confectioner. His next door neighbours were Albert, James and Frank Chart, housepainters and decorators, who also had premises in Western Road and Valence Road. The children seem to be dressed in their Sunday best: could they have been bribed by the photographer?

NOW: The cottages are, of course, little changed although most of them have been modernised and the corner shop, which did close for a time, has re-opened as a Happy Shopper.

THEN – WHITE HILL: The Elephant and Castle on White Hill was built in 1838. It is thought likely that it derives its name from the family crest (an elephant's head) of Tamplins (the brewing family who built the pub) and the inn's proximity to Lewes Castle. Just past the public house in this 1906 postcard can be seen the shop awning of J Martin, fruiterer and greengrocer, while on the corner of St John's Terrace is John Edwin Cuckney's shop (1 St Johns Terrace), then selling confectionery but later to become a fruiterer's.

NOW: Cuckney's shop, which for a short time in the 1970s was Conrad Dowding's Pet Stores, is now Lewes Videos. Mr Martin's fruit and vegetable shop at 1 Mount Pleasant was bought by EM Large in about 1957 and it continued as a fruiterer/greengrocery business until the early 1970s. Since then it has been a private residence.

THEN – ST JOHN'S TERRACE: A grid of houses for artisans was built in the Pells area. This included St Johns Terrace which originally incorporated what is now St John's Hill. The shop (number 2) was a saddler's business from the turn of the century until just before the First World War and was run by Esther Annie Young. She may have been the widow of Absolom Young, who had been a saddler at 2 Mount Pleasant before 1900. By 1914-15, it was in the ownership of William Gladstone Pelham, the first of a long line of confectioners to occupy the premises.

NOW: Sadly, the shop at number 2 that, from about 1982, was G&E Haines, Newsagent, has gone the way of so many corner shops and closed down. The shop was empty and boarded up for some time and looked very dilapidated. It is now a pine furniture business.

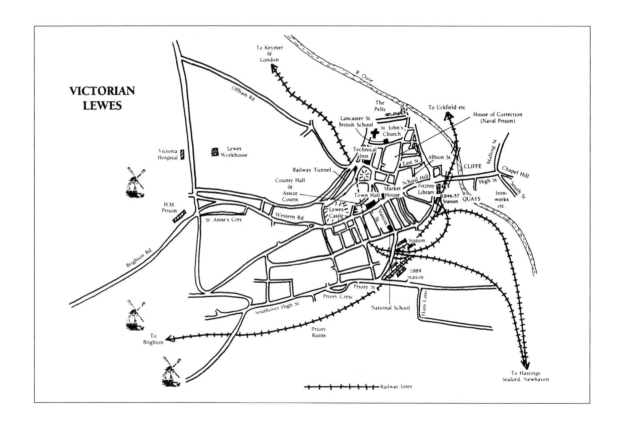

VICTORIAN LEWES

To Keymer & London

R. Ouse

Offham Rd

The Pells

To Uckfield etc.

House of Correction (Naval Prison)

Lancaster St.
British School

St. John's Church

Victoria Hospital

Lewes Workhouse

Technical Inst.

Albion St.

East St.

Malling St.

CLIFFE

Chapel Hill

Railway Tunnel

School Hill

County Hall & Assize Courts

Market House

Fitzroy Library

High St.

South St.

1846-57 Station

QUAYS

Iron-works etc.

H.M. Prison

Town Hall

Lewes Castle

St. Anne's Cres.

Western Rd

Station

Brighton Rd

Station

1889 Station

Priory St

Ham Lane

Priory Cresc.

To Brighton

Southover High St.

National School

Priory Ruins

To Hastings
Seaford, Newhaven

Railway lines

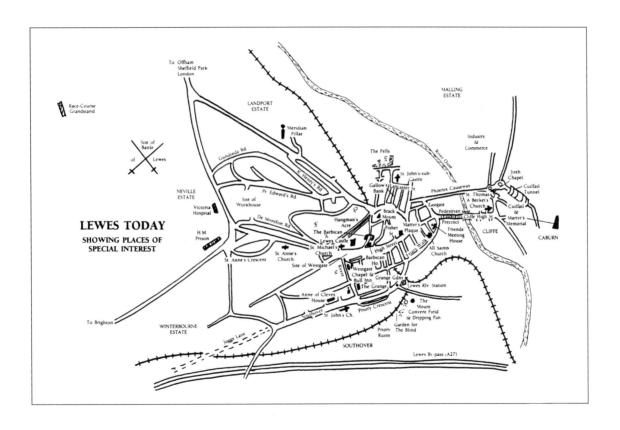

To Offham
Sheffield Park
London

Race-Course
Grandstand

Site of
Battle
of Lewes

LANDPORT
ESTATE

MALLING
ESTATE

Meridian
Pillar

Industry
&
Commerce

NEVILLE
ESTATE

Gundreds Rd

St. Henry's Rd

Pr. Edward's Rd

Site of
Workhouse

The Pells

St John's-sub-
Castro

River Ouse

Jireh
Chapel

Cuilfail
Tunnel

Victoria
Hospital

Gallows
Bank

Lancaster St

Phoenix Causeway

St. Thomas
A Becket's
Church

Cuilfail
&
Martyr's
Memorial

De Montfort Rd

Eastgate
Pedestrian
Precinct

Cliffe High St

H.M.
Prison

Hangman's
Acre

The Barbican
Lewes Castle

Brack
Mount

Fisher
St

Martyr's
Plaque

Friends'
Meeting
House

CLIFFE

CABURN

St. Michael's
Church

High Street

St. Anne's
Church

All Saints
Church

St. Anne's Crescent

Site of Westgate

Barbican
Ho.

Westgate
Chapel &
Bull Inn

Friars Walk

Keere St

Grange Gdns

The Grange

Lewes Rly Station

Anne of Cleves
House

The
Mount

Convent Field
& Dripping Pan

Garden for
The Blind

To Brighton

WINTERBOURNE
ESTATE

St John's Ch.

Southover

Priory Crescent

Priory
Ruins

Jugg Lane

SOUTHOVER

Lewes By-pass (A27)

LEWES TODAY

**SHOWING PLACES OF
SPECIAL INTEREST**

95

ABOUT THE AUTHOR

BILL Young is a former Lewes and Ringmer resident who now lives in Eastbourne. He is a retired local government officer who spent most of his career working for the emergency services – the Ambulance Services in Surrey and in Derbyshire and, latterly, the Fire Brigade in East Sussex where he ended his service as Assistant Chief Officer (Corporate Services). He was a founder member of the Ringmer History Group and, apart from local history, he counts fire brigade history, photography, classical and choral music among his interests. His first book, published in 1996, was *Line of Fire – A History of Firefighting in Lewes.*

BOB Cairns is also a local government officer and he, too, was a founder member of Ringmer History Group. His collection of local picture postcards from the Edwardian period is extensive and includes Lewes, Ringmer and most of the surrounding villages. In 1988, his book *Lewes in Old Picture Postcards* was published.